My Life at
Sweetbrier

A Life Changed by Horses

Deanie Humphrys-Dunne

Monday Creek Publishing

Ohio USA

ISBN-13: 978-0692878989
ISBN-10: 069287898X

Dedication

This book is dedicated to my family, who have always encouraged me to reach for my dreams. They believed, as I do, all things are possible if you persevere. My dad deserves special recognition for making the decision that changed my life.

Table of Contents

Chapter 1: The Big Decision.. 1
Chapter 2: The First Day of School 5
Chapter 3: The Beginning of the journey.........................11
Chapter 4: Creeping Along at a Snail's Pace.................... 17
Chapter 5: Chiefie 21
Chapter 6: Fire!...25
Chapter 7: Hello Holly...29
Chapter 8: The Next Big Decision 35
Chapter 9: The First Try..37
Chapter 10: The Anthill.. 41
Chapter 11: Hits and Misses with Jumping 43
Chapter 12: My Pony, Do All..45
Chapter 13: The Search 53
Chapter 14: Fleet Nancy..59
Chapter 15: The Debut..65
Chapter 16: Learning by Experience 69
Chapter 17: The Mystery Illness 71
Chapter 18: Preparing for the Storm...............................77
Chapter 19: The Blizzard 79
Chapter 19: Travel Trouble 83
Chapter 20: Unsettling Beginning 87
Chapter 21: Big Wins at Sleepy Village 93
Chapter 22: Big Changes and New Plans..........................97
Chapter 23: The Plan...105
Chapter 24: Together Again.. 111
Chapter 25: Spotlight..115
Chapter 26: Missing in the Storm 121
Pearls of Wisdom.. 127
Take the Quiz 129
Quiz Answers 131
About the Author 133

Chapter 1: The Big Decision

Have you ever really wanted to be able to do something, but you came across a roadblock of some kind? Maybe you're afraid of new things, or maybe you have a physical challenge. Are you going to follow your dream, or are you going to push it aside without even trying? You must make a difficult choice. Instead of taking the easy street, I changed my whole life by choosing new experiences.

What do you think I dreamed about? I wanted to ride horses. It doesn't sound like such an impossible dream, does it? I imagined feeling a horse moving under me, like we were a team, but there was an obstacle to overcome. I didn't learn to walk at the usual age because I was born two months early, weighing in at three pounds. At first, the doctors told my parents it would take time. I would catch up; but, they got worried when I still crawled around at three-years-old. Finally, they took me to a specialist who said I would never be able to walk, so they might as well accept that as being set in stone like the Ten Commandments.

Deanie at two-years-old

The doctors decided I had something called cerebral palsy. It means part of my brain was damaged when I was born, making walking more difficult. My dad, being a determined person, promptly picked me up and told the doctor where he could go with that opinion. He had a very hot, unpleasant place in mind, the opposite of Heaven.

When tears splashed down my face, Daddy made a big announcement. He said, "I'm going to teach you to ride and you'll be fine." I thought, *Daddy and I could do anything together*. I wiped the tears away and wanted to prove the doctor wrong. Daddy never accepted something as fact if he thought he could change it. He wouldn't shy away from this challenge.

I took my first wobbly steps at nearly four-years-old. At first, Daddy knelt down one step ahead of me. He said, "Come on, honey, you can do it." He stretched out his arms. I tried to move my feet, but I'd fall without going anywhere. We practiced every day. Eventually, I took one tiny step and flopped into his arms. *Hooray, we did it.* We celebrated with hugs and kisses. Gradually, Daddy moved farther away. I fell often, but I learned to get up and carry on. Daddy encouraged me to keep trying. He didn't help me get up because he wanted me to figure those things out on my own so I could manage when he wasn't with me. That was a wise choice, don't you think?

Chapter 2: The First Day of School

"Aren't you excited, honey?" Mom asked. "Tomorrow is the first day of school. You'll make new friends and learn lots of things," she continued.

"Can you stay with me when I'm at school?"

"No, you're a big girl now. You'll be fine. Besides, you'll ride on a big yellow bus."

What would the bus be like? How far away will the bus take me? Will I come home again?

The first day of school arrived. Mom hung my favorite blue

dress on the closet door. After I got dressed, she braided my light blonde hair. She tied pretty blue striped ribbons on the ends. "You look adorable, dear. You're ready for the big day. I've packed your lunch and placed it in your backpack."

I bit my lip, trying to swallow tears, but they trickled down my cheeks.

Mom and Daddy at home

"What's wrong, honey?" Mom asked.

"I'll never see you again," I wailed. "The bus will drive around forever and I won't be able to come home."

"Of course, the bus will bring you home, don't worry," Mom said, trying not to laugh. "Every day the bus driver will bring you home at the end of the day."

I took a deep breath. "I feel better now," I said, drying my tears. "I thought I'd miss you forever," I sniffled.

"Come on, I'll walk down to the end of the driveway with you. We'll wait for the bus together," Mom said.

I looked down the road for the bus. The red lights flashed when it rumbled to our driveway and rolled to a stop. Mom kissed me goodbye. I held the rail and slowly climbed the two big steps. "Bye Mom," I said, waving from the window. "I'll see you soon."

The bell rang. "It's time for recess," said our teacher, Miss Brooke. The whole class ran toward the door to get in line. I was the last one because I wasn't good at running.

"I want to play hopscotch," said Betsy. "But only with the girls who would be the best players." She chose everyone except me. I sat on the bench watching them play. *Are they going to ask me?*

Finally, I whispered, "Can I play?"

"No, you can't walk right," said Betsy. "Even babies know how to walk. Besides, you can't hop on one foot," she added, turning up her nose.

She's mean. She won't even let me try.

Mary was the only one who talked to me that day. She walked right over and said, "Hello, Deanie, my name is Mary, let's be friends."

I wouldn't have talked at all if she didn't speak first. When it was time for lunch, Mary walked with me. "I'm afraid to get my lunch. What if the ladies aren't nice?" I asked.

"It's alright, I'll get your lunch for you and bring it back to our table." Wasn't that sweet? Mary got my lunch every day. When she was absent, I sat at the table by myself, without lunch.

<hr />

At home after the first day, I said, "Mom, Betsy wouldn't let me play hopscotch at recess. Betsy said that even babies know how to walk. How nasty is that?"

"Don't worry, dear. Next time tell her you can ride horses and she can't. Maybe she'll be nicer once she gets to know you."

"Maybe, but I can't imagine her being friendly."

"Did you make any new friends?"

"Only one little girl talked to me, Mom. Her name is Mary. She sits in front of me. That little girl loves to talk. In fact, she talked so much Miss Brooke had to remind her to stop. Mary almost got sent in the hallway for talking. She asked me why I didn't get into trouble. I said it was because I only listened. Mary never asked me why I walk differently than she does. She even had lunch with me."

"I'm glad you have a new friend, dear. Mary seems like a nice little girl."

"Me too, Mom. Mary takes good care of me. Maybe she'll be a nurse when she grows up. I think she'd be good at that."

Chapter 3: The Beginning of the journey

Have you ever heard of Easton, Connecticut? It's the tiny town where I started my journey in horsemanship. I remember answering the phone one day and the caller asking, "What is Sweetbrier anyway, a vegetable farm?"

"No, it's a riding school," I said. My parents started it so my dad could keep his promise to me. When they first moved there, the buzz around town was the farm harbored a buried treasure. Mom said they looked high and low for the hidden precious objects, but the only treasure we found was the memories we have of our lives there.

What would you see if you visited Sweetbrier? You couldn't overlook the sprawling yellow Victorian style house, built in 1893. Mom said people came from far away to admire the beautiful pink "Sweetbrier Roses" the farm was named after. It took three years for the original owner to finish building the house. If you looked below the attic windows you'd see the word "Sweetbrier" beautifully etched in the wood. Across from the house was a tiny stone cottage. Sometimes people who helped take care of the horses lived there.

Sweetbrier, The Humphrys family home

Entering the second driveway you'd see the yellow barn, outdoor riding ring and rolling pastures where the horses grazed and played. Below the main barn, you'd notice a small stone barn, which was once a place where old-fashioned carriages were stored. At the top of the hillside, you'd view the big cinder block indoor arena where we rode in bad weather.

The Sweetbrier barns and riding ring

If you climbed the steps outside, you'd open the door to a mud room, where we sat to take off our boots before going into the house. Once you opened the door you'd see the biggest kitchen you could imagine. You could hold a dance in there. Other beautiful, unique things inside the house were two fireplaces. One was made of fieldstone and the other was olive-green marble. In the big dining room, with the marble fireplace, there was a built-in China cabinet where Mom displayed some colorful dishes. The China cabinet even had a hidden compartment where you could put your own treasures.

No wonder Sweetbrier was my favorite place in the whole world. It was magical; a place to build dreams.

Little Deanie

My first riding adventure happened when I was five-years-old. Why did my heart pound when Daddy led me around the riding ring on the freckled grey pony, Little Man, for the first time ever? I plodded around, listening to the steady clip-clop of Little Man's hooves hit the sandy soil of the riding ring. My legs wobbled, sliding from side to side. Isn't it amazing I didn't fall off? Daddy led me around while he rode another horse because my arms weren't strong enough to steer Little Man myself. Sometimes when I rode along on Little Man my legs got so tired I slid off. Yikes! Without warning, I sat in the dirt looking up at Little Man. I wasn't hurt but disappointed I fell off for no reason. What happened next? Could I give up? That was never an option. The family motto was, "The Humphrys don't give up." Daddy picked me up, gave me a kiss, and lifted me back on.

How could I figure out the magic formula for staying on? It was much more fun than sitting in the dirt without my pony.

Chapter 4: Creeping Along at a Snail's Pace

When I got stronger, I rode by myself. This was more complicated because I had to steer Little Man AND stay on him while we walked. It was fun to walk around practicing telling him where to go by using the reins. If the reins were part of a car, they would be the steering wheel. It took time to get used to the steady rhythm of his walk.

I learned about trotting next. Trotting is a little faster gait. I had to learn to post, which means rising up and down with the motion of the horse. It took practice, because at first I bounced around like a ball on the water. It's very bumpy and uncomfortable. But, when I got the rhythm, it seemed like dancing. *It's another thing to celebrate. Now I can post the right way. It took long enough.*

Guess what Little Man did when he got bored? He fell asleep while I rode him! I got up and said, "Daddy, Little Man went to sleep again."

I hoped giving him sugar cubes before I rode would help him behave. It didn't. He took a nap whenever he wanted one.

One day, I realized he walked slower and slower, just before he'd lie down. I squeezed the saddle with my legs, and gave him a little kick. He kept walking. It worked. Hooray! *I figured out how to keep Little Man on his feet.*

It took a long time practicing trotting before I could progress to the next thing, cantering. It is a slow gallop. Just when I mastered posting, I had to learn not to "bounce" at all when I was cantering. I needed to follow the motion of the horse. I practiced and practiced, but still I bounced around. *Why is it so tricky?*

I asked Daddy, "How long will it take before I don't bounce when I'm cantering?"

Daddy said, "It will take time, honey. Keep practicing and one day you will be able to do it perfectly."

I wondered when that day would come. Why does

everything take so long to learn? Someday I will know how to do it. I'll keep trying.

My older sister, Terri, started winning in the horse shows at five-years-old. I loved to watch her ride in them, but I wondered what it would be like to ride in shows.

"When can I compete in the shows, Daddy?" I asked.

Daddy said, "We'll keep working on strengthening your legs. You'll be able to show. You can do anything if you keep trying."

I want to win at shows, even the big ones. I'll do that someday. I'd need a special horse to get that far.

Chapter 5: Chiefie

My mom had a remarkable Arabian pony named Chiefie. An Arabian is a breed of horse. Chiefie was a handsome brown and white fellow. His looks weren't his only asset. He had brains. Daddy spent many hours training him to do tricks so he could perform at the shows. Chiefie, could lie down, count, rear up on his hind legs and even sit down on command. Isn't that amazing?

Mom and Chiefie enjoyed a special relationship, like long-time friends. She loved riding him through the woods. She trusted him to take her home safely, even if they got lost. He guided her home many times in the dark. Once when Chiefie had a horrible abscess in his throat, Mom stayed up all night holding hot compresses on it until the abscess opened and drained. By the next morning, Chiefie felt much better. He was able to munch on his hay and oats again.

Daddy knew I wanted to ride in shows, but I wasn't quite ready. He wanted to give me something special to do while I worked toward my goal of competing in shows. What would he do? He let me ride Chiefie in special performances called exhibitions.

Daddy with Chiefie playing dead

When we did exhibitions, Daddy put me on Chiefie and I'd walk, trot, and canter with him whenever Daddy gave the command. Then he'd call us into the center of the ring and lift me off before Chiefie did his tricks. The crowd always cheered wildly for us. During one exhibition, we cantered around the corner near the gate and Chiefie almost slowed down to a trot. I spoke softly to him, "Come on boy, keep going," as I squeezed him hard with my legs. He kept going. Some people in the crowd laughed and cheered when they heard what I whispered to him.

What happened if I wanted to give Chiefie a carrot when he was in his stall? I was too small to see over the top of the stall so I tapped on the door three times. It was our special signal. He walked to the front so I could see him.

One day while cantering Chiefie around the ring, I lost my balance and fell between his front legs. He stopped immediately so he wouldn't step on me. Chiefie was a hero to me because he watched out for me and cared for me every way he could. I patted his soft pink nose. When we got back to the barn, I gave him extra carrots. Don't you think he earned them?

Chapter 6: Fire!

Summer at Sweetbrier was pretty and peaceful. In early evening, Daddy worked the horses in the ring. Behind him, horses grazed happily in the fields. One evening, Terri and I watched from our bedroom window while Daddy trained one of the horses. In a heartbeat, our world changed forever. We heard a loud bang. Huge yellow flames shot through the barn roof. "Mom, call 911! The barn is burning!" Sparks flew everywhere. We froze from fear, staring at the flames.

"The firemen are coming, stay inside," Mom said.

Daddy jumped off his horse and ran toward the burning

building to rescue the horses that remained trapped. One by one he led them to safety. He had to save the privately-owned horses first. Sirens blared. The fire trucks sped up the driveway and the firemen busily sprayed the raging flames. In spite of their brave efforts, most of the barn remained covered in flames. Daddy raced in one last time, although he had suffered burns on his hands. He tried to free Chiefie and Terri's new horse, Jubilee. The heat became too intense. He couldn't loosen the latches on the doors. Chiefie and Jubilee were gone. We all felt devastated, especially Mom. She loved Chiefie so deeply.

"Are you all right? How are your hands?" We swallowed tears when we noticed burns on Daddy's hands and the fire had even burned his wavy brown hair.

"I'm all right, girls," Daddy said, hugging us tightly.

We lived in a tiny town where news spread rapidly to the residents. They rushed to our house to help in any way possible. The Dorfman family across the street, let the firemen use water from their pool to fight the huge flames engulfing our barn.

What will we do now? Will we always suffer this sadness? It's hanging over us like a heavy black cloud. Will we rebuild? Will we have the courage to start again?

The firemen stayed late into the night. They sprayed the

roof of our house in case any sparks from the fire landed there. The spray prevented the fire from spreading anywhere else.

It was hard to go outside for a long time after the fire. The smell of smoke lingered. We hated to pass the site where the barn once stood. The memories were too sad.

"Why did the fire start?" I asked.

"The hay we bought last week must not have been cured properly. That means it didn't dry long enough before it was made into bales. If it's not cured, heat from the bales can start fires."

"Daddy, what will happen now?"

"Mom and I need to decide whether we want to rebuild. It would be a huge project and expense."

"Daddy, we can't give up. The Humphrys don't give up," I reminded him. "We can build a new barn and become better than ever. Our neighbors, the Raynors, the Gillands, and the Simmonds already told you they would help."

"That's right," Daddy said. "Our neighbors are such a blessing. I think we should build a new barn. Everyone has sad things happen in their lives. We should put them behind us and move on the best we can."

It took nearly a year to build the new barn. It looked gorgeous with the bright yellow paint outside and the sturdy oak stalls inside.

Chapter 7: Hello Holly

The year after the fire, we all got a heavenly surprise. My sister Holly was born. Her birthday is near Christmas so that's how she got her name.

It was fun having a little sister. She was cute with very light blonde hair. When she got older, she had many blonde curls.

Holly was less than three-years-old when she started riding. She kept asking when she could ride our brown, fuzzy pony named Cocoa. It was astonishing to see such a tiny girl posting away on Cocoa.

Daddy punched lots of extra holes in the stirrup leathers to make them short enough for her. You could see Holly's beautiful curls peeking out from under her riding hat. Even when Holly first started riding, she had perfect leg position and posture. She showed the talents of a gifted rider.

One night when Holly was three-years-old, she rode a horse named Mister E. He liked jumping. He kept circling closer and closer to the jump until finally he cantered right over it. Holly stayed on him over the jump, but she slid off when they came to the corner. Daddy picked her up and hugged her.

"Honey, are you okay?" he asked, trying to keep calm.

"Yes," Holly answered. She only cried for a moment. Wasn't she brave?

Daddy put her back on Mister E so that she wouldn't be afraid to ride him again.

At home that night Holly was watching a story on television when Daddy came in. "I think you did fine tonight, honey. You stayed on for the jump. You did a good job."

Holly said, "How could you say that? I didn't. I falled off."

At five-years-old, Holly trained a brown and white pony

named Goldie. She was tiny, at only forty-two inches high. Goldie sailed over jumps as high as three feet.

Holly won quite a few ribbons on Goldie in pony classes. The crowds cheered for the cute Pinto pony ridden by the brave little girl with blonde braids flying.

Holly and Goldie loved to play a game called Saddle Ball. It was similar to Polo. The riders used special sticks called mallets. They tried to run to the plastic ball first and put the stick through one of the spaces in it. Then they'd race to the goal net and throw the ball into it. Every time you threw the ball into the net, you earned points. Other riders tried to snatch the ball before you made a goal. Of course, the more points you earned, the better. You need ponies who are quick and agile. Goldie was fast, so she and Holly were well-suited for the game. One day while playing Saddle Ball, Holly and Goldie got too close to the fence. Goldie slipped and fell on Holly's leg. It was swollen and sore when she limped home.

"What will happen now, Mommy?" Holly asked.

"We'll see the doctor. He'll take a picture of your leg to see if it's broken."

"Will it come out in color?" Holly felt disappointed to see it in plain black and white.

It turned out her leg was broken and she needed to wear a cast for a month. She was anxious for her leg to heal so she could ride Goldie again. She missed the fun they had together. Holly even taught Goldie to pull a little cart. Holly's friends enjoyed riding around the farm in the cart.

Holly and Goldie did another special thing. They played pony express. Holly trotted Goldie down to the house, picked up things there and brought them back to the barn. She could carry snacks, books, or anything she wanted. She attached a saddlebag to her saddle to hold her treasures.

Holly and Goldie jumping in a show at Sweetbrier

A tall stone hitching post stood outside the front entrance to our house. It had a built-in ring meant for tying horses. At the bottom, there was the letter M, made from pebbles, built into the cement. The M stood for Merit, the last name of the original owners of Sweetbrier.

One day Holly rode Goldie to the town Post Office. Guess what happened? The next day their picture was in the paper.

When Holly was about eight-years-old she became interested in art. She took lessons from a famous local artist named Ray Quinley. One of her first oil paintings was of our family Bible. It took many hours for Holly to complete it. Mom still has it hanging in her home.

Deanie Humphrys-Dunne

Chapter 8: The Next Big Decision

The first shows I entered were a disappointment. I went into "horsemanship" classes. In those events, the judges chose the winners by their "form," or how they looked on the horse. *Did I have my heels down? Was I sitting straight? Were my legs still?* There were many things to consider. I didn't win in these classes because the other riders had closer to perfect positions. My legs wiggled and keeping my heels down was always a challenge. *It's not fair. I practice every day and still don't win. If I worked harder than other kids, why didn't I win?*

After I mastered cantering, I made a monumental decision. I'm going to ask Daddy to teach me to jump. He'll listen. I know he will. I started building my case, like someone facing a jury for the first time.

"Daddy, I want you to teach me to jump," I announced. I think he was a little surprised, so he pondered the request carefully.

"I'm not sure that's a good idea, honey. You'll probably fall off a lot," he said.

"That's not fair. You always said I could do anything I wanted if I tried. Besides, you even taught a blind person to jump, so if he can do it, why can't I?" *Yes, I have him now*, I thought. *He won't have a defense.*

Daddy said, "All right, we'll give it a try. But you know it's going to take time to learn."

"I don't mind, Daddy. If I fall off, I'll get up, just as I've always done. I don't care if it takes a long time. Someday I'll know how to jump and I'll compete in shows, you'll see."

Chapter 9: The First Try

Daddy decided we'd try jumping to see if my legs were strong enough to handle it. I tossed around in my bed the night before, thinking of what might happen.

I wonder what it will feel like. *Will it be bouncy? Will it be too hard to stay on?*

"Daddy, who will I ride for my first jump? Can I ride Cocoa because we already know each other?"

"I think Cocoa would be fine. She's a pony so she's not too tall and you're already used to her stride," he said.

The next morning, I brushed Cocoa's furry coat and put the saddle and bridle on her. "Today we're going to jump, Cocoa. Do what you can to help me stay on." I pretended she understood. It built my confidence.

Daddy lifted me on Cocoa and we got ready for the first jump.

"Daddy, you remember today is the day Cocoa and I are going to jump, right?"

"Yes, honey. I'm going to set up the crossrail right now."

"Don't make it too high, Daddy. It's the first time, you know." I wouldn't let him forget that.

"I'll make it just the right size," Daddy said.

I felt my heart pounding. My hands were cold, despite the fact that the temperature was seventy-five degrees outside.

It's so high. I didn't think it would look this scary. What happens if I fall off? Don't be silly. It is not as if we are going to jump the Empire State Building.

"Are you ready, honey?"

"I guess so," I said, trying to ignore the lump in my throat. I trotted Cocoa toward the jump, holding my breath. As soon as her front feet hit the ground, I slid off. My legs weren't strong enough to hold me on.

Daddy picked me up, giving me a gentle hug. I got back on and tried again, but with the same result.

"You tried hard to stay on, sweetie," Daddy said. "I'm proud of you for getting back on after you fell twice; nevertheless, I think we should wait another year to give your muscles a chance to strengthen. We're not going to give up, but I think it's better to wait."

I walked Cocoa back into the barn. I patted her neck. "It's not your fault, girl. You took the jump."

I felt like a failure. It seemed like I was giving up, but Daddy knew best. I'd have to wait and see. Tears streamed down my cheeks.

"Daddy, are you sure we can't try again tomorrow?" I begged.

"I think it's best to wait, honey," he said. "The time will pass quickly. I'll let you know when I think you're ready to try again."

Chapter 10: The Anthill

About a year later Daddy said he'd been watching me ride and my legs were more secure.

"I think you're ready to try jumping again," he said.

I hopped up and down with excitement. "Daddy, do you mean it?"

"Of course," he said. "I wouldn't tease you about that." I kept wondering what it would feel like to jump. *Would I stay on this time? Would we have to wait for my legs to strengthen again?*

The big day finally arrived. I was going to jump Fair Lad.

41

His nickname was Laddie. He was a big, white horse, with blue eyes. He was a reliable jumper, always relaxed, no matter what happened. The big fellow liked to eat everything in sight. Once Laddie chewed someone's straw hat and even nibbled on a watch. Isn't that funny? Did he have goats in his family tree? He loved drinking orange soda. He slurped it right out of the bottle. It was a good thing nothing scared Laddie because on my first day jumping, I felt anxious enough for both of us. I looked at the tiny crossrail jump, convinced it looked as high as Pike's Peak.

I can't do this. Yikes! It's too high. I took a deep breath and told myself to get a grip. How can I jump Pike's Peak if I can't focus on what to do? Besides, if I can't handle this, I won't get to the next step.

"Couldn't you make it lower, Daddy?" I pleaded.

"If I did, there'd be nothing to jump," he answered.

My legs trembled and my hands felt cold as I turned toward the jump, holding my breath. Laddie hopped over the little thing, barely noticing it.

"Daddy, I jumped!" I hollered. He gave me kisses and hugs to congratulate me. Looking back, I realize I've seen anthills higher than that jump. I'm surprised Laddie didn't need glasses to help him see it. *This is easier than I thought. I'll be able to jump in shows in no time.*

Chapter 11: Hits and Misses with Jumping

It seemed like Laddie and I didn't always communicate well. There's a lot more to this jumping stuff than I thought. It's a matter of timing. When I expected him to take the jump, he'd run around it. Splat, I was on the ground. If I got ready for another stride before he jumped, he'd leave it out and I'd fall off. Sometimes Laddie would stop in front of the jump and I'd go over it. *I'm not supposed to be jumping by myself. Laddie and I should be in the same place.* It was not what I had in mind, for sure. I was not spending much time ON the horse. *Why didn't I fall off gracefully? No matter how much practice I got, it seemed I was in the air for a few seconds before landing, with a thud. I'd rather find the secret to staying on the horse.*

After six years of practicing every day I started jumping in shows. What happened the first time? I was so nervous I took two extra jumps. It's called being "off course." The course was simple, just four jumps, twice around the ring, I ended in the wrong place because I took two extra jumps. It was embarrassing because the official yelled "Off course" and everyone noticed. *Well, at least I didn't fall off the first time I jumped in a show.*

Chapter 12: My Pony, Do All

You might wonder why even as a teenager, I always called my father, "Daddy." I tried thinking of him as "Dad," but it just wasn't comfortable. It didn't seem to fit, so he remained "Daddy" in our conversations.

There's an interesting story connected to my pony, Do All. Daddy had a friend who bought and sold horses. His name was Mr. Emerson. Whenever Mr. Emerson had a horse or pony he thought Daddy would like, he'd call him. One day Mr. Emerson said, "I've got a pony you're going to love. He's gentle as a lamb and has great manners."

Daddy said, "I can come by to see him tomorrow."

"Daddy, can I come too?" I asked.

"Sure, I'd love company for the trip and Mr. Emerson would enjoy seeing you."

"Goody, I can't wait."

Daddy hitched the trailer to the pickup truck and off we went to visit Mr. Emerson.

When we got there, Mr. Emerson was waiting for us in the barn. He said, "Hey, it's great to see you. It's been a while."

"We're glad to see you, too. Where's the pony you wanted to show us?"

"He's in the stall at the end of the aisle on the right." Daddy led the pony out of the stall. He studied the pony's eye. The pony was medium size with stripes on his legs and a brown stripe down his back. He had a blaze and he was a tan color called buckskin. Maybe one of his relatives was part zebra. I'd never seen stripes like that.

"He's cute, don't you think, Daddy?"

"Yes, he is. Can one of your daughters hop on him so we can see him being ridden?" Daddy asked.

"Sure, Dana is out by the ring. She'll be back in a minute." Dana got the pony ready and rode him in the ring. He behaved well, but Mr. Emerson must've thought he needed something else to seal the deal. He said, "If you don't think he's gentle, watch this. Dana, get off and give me the reins, please." Mr. Emerson took the reins from Dana and walked the pony over to his house, and up three steps, into the living room! You can imagine the shock on his wife's face.

"Get that pony out of here this minute!" she yelled.

"Okay, dear, I wanted to prove a point." He turned the pony around and out the door they went.

"Well, that certainly was a surprise," Daddy said. "Why don't we talk about the price?" Daddy and Mr. Emerson discussed the price and made a deal.

When they finished everything, Daddy led the pony into the trailer and we headed home.

Back at home, we told Mom all about the new pony. She laughed when Daddy said Mr. Emerson took the horse into the house.

We often asked Mom to name the new horses and ponies. She had a wonderful imagination and came up with good names for them. "What should we name him, Mom?" After a minute or two she said, "How about Do All? He's already done something remarkable, don't you think?"

"Good idea, Mom. That name fits him," I said.

Do All was a fine pony. We called him Doey for short. We used him to teach kids to ride. He was so responsive even little children loved him. After we had him a while, I started jumping him. He seemed to know what to do when he saw a jump. He rarely refused. Doey sailed over anything he faced.

Doey's style of jumping was unique. He "danced" just before the jump, moving left and then right. Sometimes when we entered the Pony Hunter Classes, we didn't win because the judge didn't like his style.

Doey and me outside the indoor arena

One day we decided to enter a show close to home. Doey and I got a sixth place in one of the pony classes where you don't jump. We wanted to compete in the Pony Jumper Class. It's judged on whether you clear the jumps or not. Style doesn't matter. Whichever horse and rider has the least number of faults wins. There's a four-fault penalty for a knockdown and three faults if your horse refuses the jump.

I walked over to the secretary's tent to enter the Pony Jumper Class. The secretary said, "I'm sorry, Deanie. We only have one other pony entered in the class. If you want to compete, you'll have to ride against the horses."

"Um, I guess I can do that. Here's the entry fee." I walked back to the ring to tell Daddy what happened.

"You can handle it, honey. Doey won't worry and neither should you."

"Okay, Daddy. The class is starting. I'll watch a few riders take the course so I know it."

The announcer said, "Our next competitor is number 15, Do All, ridden by Deanie Humphrys. This is one of the ponies entered."

I kissed Daddy for luck and rode into the ring. I cantered briskly toward the first jump. We flew over it. Doey took every jump without knocking it down or refusing. I patted his neck and smiled. Daddy cheered and whistled from the ringside.

"Great job, sweetie," he said. "Now we'll wait and see how the other riders do."

We waited a while until the announcer said, "This is the last contestant."

"Good, now we'll see if we have a jump off." About two minutes after that, the announcer said, "Ladies and gentlemen, we have a tie between number 15, Do All and number 120, Sunny. Do you want to jump or toss a coin?"

"Jump," I yelled.

"I'm glad you chose that. I'd rather you earn your ribbon," Daddy said.

"Daddy, I'll go first. The course is the same, only higher." He kissed me.

I whispered, "Okay, Doey, let's try our best." I hope he listened.

"Ladies and gentlemen, our first horse for the jump off is "Do All, ridden by Deanie Humphrys."

We galloped toward the first jump. Everything was fine. We kept going, one by one, we flew over the jumps. The last jump was the barrel jump. It looked huge from down here. I think it's four feet high, yikes. I squeezed him hard with my legs, trying to urge him forward. He touched the rail with his front hooves. It wobbled but stayed up. *We made it, I can' t believe it.* I patted Doey's neck and kissed one of his braids. "Good job, boy. We'll know who wins soon."

"Ladies and gentlemen, our next horse is Sunny, ridden by Penny Stanton."

I watched them jump the course, holding my breath. They

came to the barrel jump. He knocked it down. Oh my gosh, we won!

Daddy clapped and cheered. He hugged me when we left the ring. "I'm super proud of you," Daddy said.

A photographer took my picture. We made the headlines the next day.

Doey and me at a show

Chapter 13: The Search

When I turned eighteen, I couldn't ride Doey in competitions anymore because that was the age limit. Did I have a plan? Yes, I wanted Daddy to look for a special horse who could compete in the big shows. I started my campaign. "Daddy, you can sell Doey and use some of that money to buy my new horse," I said. I even babysat for a neighbor's children and gave Daddy fifty dollars toward the horse of my dreams. I was teaching at Sweetbrier then and I knew Daddy wanted to take a trip across the country.

"Daddy, because you're going to take a trip anyway, why

don't you look for my horse? I'll stay and tach while you're looking."

He said, "Okay, that's what we'll do."

I spent my spare time wondering what my new horse would look like. Would it be chestnut? (reddish) Would it be gray? Would it be shiny black like the horse Daddy and I saw once at a show? He told me that day he wanted me to have a horse that would stand out. What if he didn't find it?

<hr />

Daddy drove down the driveway with the two-horse trailer attached to his camper. He called every week with updates. I asked, "Daddy, did you find my horse yet?" He told me stories of the horses he saw and didn't choose. Would he find exactly the right one? I didn't know for sure, but I knew Daddy had a gift. He had an intuition for choosing horses. When he had that feeling, he was rarely wrong. I felt confident he wouldn't make a mistake choosing my horse. It was too important and he knew exactly the kind of horse I needed. He'd look for a horse with talent, looks, and the perfect temperament. It won't be easy to find this combination, but if anyone can succeed, Daddy could.

We were busy at the farm, but still the time seemed to drag by. I wondered what Daddy was doing each day. *Is Daddy still looking for my horse? Is he on his way home with it? Is he coming home without it? I tried to imagine what I would do if he didn't find it. That was too sad. Instead, I imagined he found the perfect horse.* How exciting is that?

Finally, the camper and the trailer rumbled into the driveway. I ran to Daddy, showering him with hugs and kisses.

"Daddy, did you find my horse?" I asked excitedly. He recited information on all the horses he didn't choose. "I almost chose a Palomino, but I didn't have the intuition. I knew he wasn't the right one," he said.

I stood on my tiptoes and looked in the trailer. There was no horse. I could feel myself crumbling, thinking there was no special horse after all. Tears welled up in my eyes.

It seemed like forever before Daddy said, "I saw another horse in Ohio. She's a black Thoroughbred, four-years-old. I bought her, but she's still in Ohio because she got hurt in a trailer accident. She fell through the floor on her way to a show. She has scrapes and cuts, but she'll be all right. The owner of the farm, Mr. Landon, put her on a lunge line to show me what she could do. She galloped over a three-foot jump with no hesitation. Boy, does she have style. I got goosebumps watching her. I think she's the one for you."

"What else do you know about her, Daddy? Did she race?"

"She started training as a racehorse, but she wasn't fast enough. Mr. Landon recognized that and started teaching her to jump instead."

"When is she coming?" I asked, holding my breath.

"She'll probably come in a few days. The owner will call me when she's healed more."

I wished I were with her already. The accident must've been horrible for her. I wanted to put medicine on her cuts so she'll feel better.

"Daddy, what's her name?" I asked, hugging him tightly.

"Gee, I forgot to ask," he said.

How could you meet someone and not know her name? That is strange.

About a week later, we got the call from Mr. Landon. We learned my horse would be transported to Porter, New York, where we'd pick her up with our trailer. As you can imagine, I couldn't wait for the big day. When it finally came, we went to the exit and didn't see the horse van. Someone on a motorcycle came along and asked, "Are you looking for a horse van?"

Daddy said, "Yes."

"Follow me, I'll take you to the horse van," the man said.

We drove through more winding roads. *Will we ever get there?*

By the time we located the van, it was getting dark. I hurried up the ramp and patted my horse's soft coat. I looked at her halter. The brass nameplate on the halter said Fleet Nancy.

Look how sleek and pretty she is. *Will she walk on our trailer? Maybe she's worried about the accident; but she walked right on. She showed us she had courage.*

Chapter 14: Fleet Nancy

When Fleet Nancy came home, I unwrapped the bandages protecting her legs. I walked her into the stall. She looked in the feed bin for her oats.

"Don't worry, Nancy, I know you're hungry after the long trip. I'll get your dinner. In the meantime, munch on your hay," I said, patting her neck. When I poured the oats into the bin, she nibbled on them eagerly.

I wanted her to know I was her friend, so I got up early to feed and groom her. *I remember giving Little Man the sugar cubes to improve his behavior. It didn't help. This time I hoped for a better result.* She settled in to her new home for a few days before I rode her. I put salve on her cuts several times a day. Nancy stood quietly while I treated her. I think she realized I wanted to help her feel better.

Things were a little rocky the first day I rode Nancy. Several weeks had passed since the accident. The cuts on her back were healed, but Daddy used a special saddle pad with extra foam in it to make sure she was comfortable.

Fleet Nancy seemed to pay attention to me when I wanted her to trot. I'd squeeze the saddle with my legs and she'd instantly start trotting. But I had trouble getting her to canter. I told her to canter, using my leg and rein as a signal, but she kept trotting. Once she understood the signal, she zoomed around the ring like a black blur. I felt frustrated because she galloped around, instead of the relaxed canter I wanted. *I wonder how long it will take before we get it right. What if it's always a problem?*

While I walked down the path toward the house, tears trickled down my cheeks. When I entered the house, Mom said, "What's wrong, honey?"

I sniffled, "Nancy doesn't like me."

"Don't be silly. Of course, she does. You need to get used to each other." Mom understood how much I loved Nancy. She knew my single passion was for Nancy and I to become a winning team.

"Maybe we need more practice," I said, feeling the lump in my throat.

The next week we started jumping. My hands were cold even though it was hot out. My legs trembled. The jump was two and a half feet high. I steered Nancy toward it, holding my breath. *This looks scary. What will happen? Will she stop? Will she be afraid?* We cantered toward the jump. *Whew! We made it.* I patted her neck. She earned extra carrots that night.

A few days later Daddy decided it was time to take bigger jumps. He set up a barrel jump about three feet high. This looks scary. *What will happen? Will she stop? Will she be afraid?* We cantered toward the jump. *Whew! We made it, but we could have done it without the last stride she snuck in.* I patted her neck. She earned extra carrots that night.

"Try it once more, honey. You can do better," Daddy said.

We galloped toward the jump, but this time Nancy almost stopped. At the last minute, she jumped, but I fell off. She cantered around the ring without me.

"Are you okay, honey?"

I bit my lower lip, swallowing tears. "I guess so."

Daddy caught Nancy while I brushed myself off.

This time we circled around toward the jump and she took it right in stride. I patted her silky neck. "Good job, Nancy. Too bad we couldn't have done that the first time. Think of all the drama we would have missed."

I could feel the tears drying on my face when I went home that night. I walked into the kitchen and Mom noticed the sadness in my puffy blue eyes.

"What's wrong, honey?" Mom asked.

"I fell off today. I thought Nancy was going to take the jump, but she almost stopped and then jumped. Maybe she's trying to show me she doesn't like me," I sniffled.

"Don't be silly. You've only had her a few weeks. You need more time to work together. Give yourself more time."

"Well, you might be right," I said, pretending to be

confident.

Nancy and I spent all the time we could together. Every day I brushed her from head to toe. I studied the kind expression in her large, brown eyes. Daddy said a horse's eyes are important. If the horse has small eyes, it has a nasty disposition.

We worked on our signals so Nancy knew when I wanted her to canter. We didn't jump every day because that would strain her legs. Besides, I wanted jumping to be fun for her so we scheduled time for her to relax.

Chapter 15: The Debut

Holly gave Nancy a special nickname. One day when she stood behind her, Holly said, "She has nice, round jumping muscles that remind me of a peach. How cool is that?" From then on, we all called her Peach. It seemed to suit her well.

Peach and I practiced for a year before we made our debut in the shows. We entered a small show at the Hunter's Club.

First, we had to get ready for the show. I washed her and braided her mane. She knew something special was coming. Do you know how we could tell? She curled her upper lip whenever she was excited. We could hear the little noise when she flapped it. I bet she could hardly wait for tomorrow.

Of course, I had trouble sleeping before the big day. I tried to fall asleep, but I thought about the next day and wondered what would happen. *Would I stay on for the jumps? Would I know the course? Would I be too nervous to think? Would I go off course?*

My sister Terri drove the trailer to the show. We arrived early so we could practice the jump course. Peach did her best if we could practice first. She was happy when she jumped. She hopped up and down at the end of the course. Those little hops are called crow hops. Funny word, isn't it? Can you imagine little crows hopping around trying to imitate Peach?

We tried to keep her comfortable all day. It was summer. We sponged her off with cool water after she worked. Speaking of water, we learned something surprising. Peach wouldn't drink water from other places. She only liked the water from home. After that day, we brought our own water with us. She was a diva already, don't you think?

We did another special thing for Peach. Every time she went to a show, I brought extra pieces of carrots for her. Peach loved the yummy carrot snacks and she'd sniff my pockets for them.

When it came time for our class, Open Hunters, I was jittery. My legs shook. I studied the course and watched other riders gallop around the well-maintained field. Our turn came. We circled toward the first jump. It was perfect. One by one, we took the jumps in stride. At the end, Peach celebrated with her little crow hops, pushing her neck against my hand when I patted her. She did that when she knew she'd done her best. I was so anxious; I wasn't sure how we did. You can imagine how I felt when the announcer called our number first. First prize at our first show. How amazing is that?

"We won," I said, patting Peach's shiny black neck. I kissed her soft brown nose. The judge put the blue ribbon on her bridle while she flapped her lip. I rubbed my hand on the ribbon, and the silver dish to make sure it was real.

I walked Peach back to the trailer. Mr. Bentley, the manager of the Hunter's Club said, "Hey, where did your dad find that horse? She's nice. By the way, I saw you jump. I'm impressed."

"Thanks, Mr. Bentley. Daddy bought her in Ohio." *Oh, this is the biggest compliment I've ever gotten. Imagine me getting a compliment from Mr. Bentley.*

I called Daddy after our class to tell him how we did. "Daddy, we won our class."

He liked to tease me and he said, "Is that the best you could do?"

"I think so." I sported the widest smile, thinking of our victory.

I wrapped Peach's delicate legs with soft blue bandages, and walked her on the trailer for the ride home.

When we got home, Peach savored extra oats with carrots on top. I rubbed her legs with special liniment. We needed to protect those pretty legs of hers for a long time to come. "Peach, I'm going to write to Mr. Landon to tell him you're a champion. I bet he'll be proud." She was the star today. Peach wanted to show people she loved jumping. Will she be the talk of the town?

Chapter 16: Learning by Experience

Have your parents ever told you experience is the best teacher? People can give you their opinion on how to compete in shows, but you need your own successes and failures. For example, I took Peach to a show in Farrington, Connecticut, where the jump course had some jumps higher than others. Peach and I were galloping around the course when we approached a wooden stonewall. I had to make a split-second decision. I couldn't tell which side was three inches higher, so I took the lower side and heard the dreaded words blaring over the loud speaker, "Off course." Daddy happened to be at that show. I knew he was not happy by looking into his blue eyes. They were huge to begin with, but when he was upset, they grew larger by the minute.

"Couldn't you see that you should have taken the jump on the left?" he asked.

"I had trouble telling which side was left," I complained. "I was nervous, I didn't notice which one was higher," I said, sniffling back tears.

I hated disappointing Daddy, especially when I did an embarrassing thing like taking the wrong jump. *Going off course is awful. I feel silly.*

After that experience, I studied the courses more carefully, taking note of all the small details. In addition, I watched other riders take the course first so there was no doubt about the sequence of the jumps. I only jumped first if I was absolutely sure about the course.

Chapter 17: The Mystery Illness

One morning I walked into the barn expecting to get Peach ready to ride. I opened the stall door. "Hi, Peach."

When I led her out of the stall, she could barely put weight on her front legs. I called Daddy with the terrible news.

"I'll come right away," he said. "Her legs are swollen. Let's call Dr. Howard to take a look at her."

Tears rolled down my cheeks. "Don't worry, honey, Dr. Howard will be here soon," Daddy said, giving me a hug.

I paced the floor, until I saw Dr. Howard's tan truck

rumbling up to the barn. "Hi, everyone. Let's have a look at her." He studied the inflammation in her legs. He took a blood test and a sample of the oats and hay to test for anything that might make her sick.

"I'm not sure what is causing the problem, but while I'm testing her food, soak her legs in buckets of ice water. I'll call in a day or two. Please let me know if there's any change in her condition."

"I'll take good care of her, doctor," I said.

"Thanks for coming so quickly," Daddy said.

I led Peach outside and tied the lead rope around a sturdy post outside of the indoor ring. I lifted each leg and placed it in the rubber buckets. Things went smoothly for the first few minutes. Then Peach moved one foot to the edge. While I tried to move her foot, the bucket tipped over. Water and ice splashed everywhere. Peach was startled. She pulled back hard, snapping the rope. She hobbled back to her stall, after knocking me down and stepping on my leg. *Great, Peach must've wanted both of us to have sore legs*. I got up, limped back to the barn, locked her stall door and went home to tend to my leg.

I climbed the back steps with a stiff left leg. I opened the kitchen door. "What happened, dear?" Mom asked.

"Well the short version is, I was soaking Peach's legs in ice water. She was tied to the pole outside the arena. She got scared, broke loose, knocked me down and stepped on my leg."

"Oh, I'm sorry, dear. Let's have a look." Mom rolled up my pantleg and peeked at my leg. "It's bruised and swollen. Let's put some ice on it. It'll feel better soon."

"Thanks for fixing me up, Mom. I need to get back to the barn with more ice for Peach."

"Here, honey, take this ice bag for Peach and be careful. We'll need to use the ice pack again when you get back."

"I will, Mom. It was a freak thing. Peach won't do it again."

"I carried the ice bag through the barn and dumped the ice in the buckets outside, before filling them with water. It was time to put Peach's feet in the buckets again. I didn't tie her anywhere. Instead, I held the lead rope while I picked up each front foot and put them in the center of the buckets. Peach stood perfectly until the ice was melted. She seemed happy to be going back to her stall. "Good girl, Peach. You behaved perfectly this time. I'm proud of you," I said, patting her soft neck.

⋘⟐⟑⟐⋙

After a week of soaking her feet, Dr. Howard came back to check on Peach. I walked her out on the floor and she wasn't limping. She stood on the barn floor flapping her lip. "I bet you're anxious to get back to work, aren't you, Peach?" he said.

"Deanie, I didn't find anything wrong with the hay or the oats you've been giving her. I have no idea what caused the sickness. Let me check her feet." Doctor Howard picked up Peach's front hooves and pinched the bottom of each hoof with a special tool. Peach drew her foot away from him. Daddy came in to see what was happening.

"Hi Doc, how is she doing?" Daddy asked.

"She's looking much better. The swelling is gone in her legs, but the soles of her hooves are still sensitive. I'd say she can go back to work, but you should have the blacksmith put leather pads under her shoes to protect her feet."

"That's good news, doctor. We'll call if she has any problems once she has the pads on."

"Good job, Peach. No more buckets of ice water. My leg is much better too. Both of us are ready for work," I said, kissing her soft nose. "Here, have a carrot to celebrate, Peach." She crunched on the carrot and headed back to her stall.

Peach seemed comfy with her new pads and shoes. I rode into the ring on the first day with her pads. "Peach, you're snorting and carrying on." She shook her head. "I can see you're happy to be working." I smiled, patting her neck.

Chapter 18: Preparing for the Storm

New England winters can test your patience. I hated the cold, but it's part of living in that area. Many times, the snowstorms weren't noteworthy; but some make the record books.

"It was crazy busy in the grocery store. It looks like everyone in town is shopping before the storm," Mom said. She unloaded bags of groceries. She checked the inventory; extra batteries, candles, matches and things we could eat if we lost electricity. She had the radio on all day for the latest weather updates. Weathermen insisted the storm of the century was on the way. What if they were right?

"Daddy, if we get lots of snow, how will we take care of the horses?" I asked.

"We'll find a way. We always do. Don't worry, honey."

Daddy, and I went to the barn. The horses whinnied when they saw us. Daddy threw extra sections of hay to each horse and I put the warmest blankets on each horse. I unrolled the hose and filled each horse's bucket with clean water.

"Peach, here's some new water for you," I said. She took a big sip and dribbled most of it all over my gloves. My fingers were freezing, but I thought it would be worse without my gloves so left them on.

All of the stalls were neat and clean before we headed down the path back to the house. "We've done what we can to make the horses comfortable," Daddy said. "We'll see what tomorrow brings. Thanks for helping with the horses, honey. You did a great job and helped us get ready for the storm. I couldn't have managed without you."

"You're welcome, Daddy. I'm glad we're all set for what-ever happens tomorrow."

Just thinking of all the snow they're predicting is scary. It would be nice if the weathermen were wrong. How will we get to the horses.

Chapter 19: The Blizzard

I looked out the bedroom window. The wind howled. Snow swirled furiously in every direction. I couldn't see the barn or the other buildings. Our old house creaked from the force of the wind. Standing near the window, I felt small amounts of cold air seeping in. I thought our house was like the great outdoors, but with a few less breezes. Our house was loaded with charm, but those chilly drafts couldn't be ignored during the winter.

Mom and Daddy sat at the breakfast table. I sat down next to them. Daddy said, "We have to work together today,

Deanie, because your sisters are away. The horses must be fed and cared for. I've been out early this morning trying to carve a path in the snow, but it snowed like mad. I'm sure the path is covered. Deanie, I already took care of the horses in the stone barn, but you and I will work together in the main stable. I know it's hard for you to walk in the deep snow and drifts, but I have a plan. I'm going to tie you to me with a rope. You'll be safe that way. We'll get to the barn together," Daddy added.

I put three layers of heavy clothes on along with my highest rubber boots. I added my hat and slipped into my gloves. I felt like a mummy all wrapped up with so many clothes, I could barely move.

Daddy got the heavy rope from the mud room. I looked out the door. Guess where the drifts were? They reached past the basement door and up to the kitchen windows.

We went back out to the mudroom and Daddy tied the rope around my waist. I held the railing, going down the steps, slowly and carefully so I didn't slip. "We're all set for our adventure now. Here we go," I said.

I stepped in the snow. It was past my waist. I walked a few feet and fell. Snow snuck under my gloves. My wrists were freezing. "Daddy, stop!" I yelled. I fell. "Wait until I get up. Okay, now we can keep going."

"Good job, honey, you're doing great. We don't have that much further to go," Daddy hollered. I barely heard him because of the noisy wind.

Finally, we reached the door to the barn. Daddy pushed it hard to slide it open. Hooray we made it. *I felt like a pioneer.* When the door opened, the horses went nuts. They whinnied and stomped their hooves on the ground. Some kicked the sides of their stalls. They made quite a racket. They acted like they were about to starve.

"Settle down, guys. We know you're hungry," Daddy said.

He hurried up the ladder to the hayloft and started throwing sections of hay through the overhead trap doors into the stalls. We heard the horses munching on their hay, instead of stomping their feet, a big improvement in the noise level.

"Start watering the horses, honey, while I feed the horses their oats."

"Okay, Daddy." I uncoiled the hose and pulled it down the aisle. The first three horses had only a little water, but at least it wasn't a block of ice. They slurped the water up quickly. I came to Peach's stall and discovered a block of ice in the pail. I took it off the wall and over to the sink. Bang, bang, the ice chunks fell into the sink. My gloves were soaked. The hose never failed to leak around the nozzle on the coldest days. After I finished filling Peach's bucket, I pulled the hose to the rest of the stalls and finally reached the last one. I can't remember being this glad to see the last water bucket.

Daddy fed the last horse in the aisle. He cleaned the stalls. "Let's get ready to walk back home. At least it stopped snowing and the wind is not as strong as before."

Daddy wrapped the water pipes so they wouldn't freeze. He tied the rope around me again. "We're all set, honey. The horses are comfy now." We headed for the door. Daddy opened it and snow flew into our faces. *Yuck, I hate winter. It's plain uncomfortable.*

Daddy trudged along, battling the wind and snow, towing me behind him. Reaching the steps outside the house seemed a huge feat. I clutched the rail and climbed the steps. I took off my snowy boots in the mudroom.

"Mom, I'm so glad to see you. It's good to be home," I said, giving her a long embrace.

"Me too, honey. I'm happy to have everyone back home safely."

Chapter 19: Travel Trouble

We planned to go to a show close to home. This was our first show since Peach's mysterious illness. I was up early checking Peach's braids and inspecting her glossy black coat. We were taking some of the students, so we needed the big van instead of the trailer. We were running late because some of our riders arrived later than they planned. Peach had a stall on the left side of the van. On that day, I didn't bandage her legs, thinking it would be a short trip and she'd be all right.

The trip seemed uneventful. We didn't hear any commotion when we followed behind the van. But she must've lost her balance and fallen, during the trip. When Peach walked off the truck, her hind legs were scraped and bloody. One look at them told me we were not showing. *Whenever anything happened to Peach my whole world fell apart. I blamed myself for not bandaging her legs.* I walked her to the veterinarian, Dr. Howard, who worked at the show.

Dr. Howard noticed I was crying and said, "Don't worry, Deanie. She'll be fine. It's a long way from her heart." That was his way of saying it wasn't serious. He washed her legs and put red medicine on them. "Give her a few days off until these cuts heal. Be sure to keep them clean. Take this bottle home with you."

⁂

Peach relaxed at home. I put the gooey red medicine on Peach's legs for about a week. I took her outside to graze in the field. She loved munching on the grass. Daddy was puzzled over what happened to Peach, so he called Dr. Howard to discuss it.

Dr. Howard said, "Some horses have balance problems, related to the inner ear. They need more space to keep their balance when they travel. If you tie her in the center of the horse van, she can use her legs to balance herself. When she's in the trailer, take out the center partition so she has more room. I think this will solve the problem."

We took Dr. Howard's advice and Peach never had another incident with her custom travel arrangements. I didn't send her to show without bandages again.

Chapter 20: Unsettling Beginning

I wanted Daddy to take me to a show at the Washington Riding Club, but we heard the course was tricky.

"Daddy, can we go to Washington Riding Club this weekend? I heard the outside course was hard. What do you think?"

"I'll take you on the Friday before the show so you and Peach can practice. We'll see how it goes."

"Oh, thank you Daddy." I hopped up and down thinking of going to the practice session. "We'll practice and that'll build my confidence."

Peach was her usual happy self during practice. The steep hills on the field didn't bother either of us. We decided to enter the show. When we finished practicing the course, Daddy helped boost my confidence. He said, "If you do as well as that on Sunday, you'll be hard to beat."

Wouldn't that be exciting? I know there will be some well-known riders here Sunday. I'd love to help them notice Peach.

⋘◈◈⋙

It was the morning of the show. I wrapped Peach's legs with her blue bandages, and walked her on the trailer. We arrived at the show in about half an hour. Daddy backed Peach off the trailer and put her saddle and bridle on. We rode over to the field to practice the jumps before the show started.

The course was crowded with horses and riders practicing before the start of the show. Peach and I headed toward the in and out, a double jump with only one stride between. We had a little miscommunication when she slid to a stop before the first jump and I fell off, landing on my cheek. It stung. I could feel it beginning to puff up. Meanwhile, Peach galloped off the field while the announcer shouted, "Loose horse."

Everyone gawked at the horse running loose without its rider. I wish I had somewhere to hide. It was strange Peach would run away if I fell off because of something she did; but if I fell off when it wasn't her fault, she'd stand still, looking down at me wondering what happened. Of course, I had to get back on and try again. This time it was successful, so we rested before our class. *I must not think of the fall before the next class. If I do, we might not do our best. We can do it.*

It was our turn to jump. I was nervous, but I watched other riders jump the course. We galloped toward the first jump and Peach jumped it perfectly. You couldn't see us as Peach galloped toward the lowest part of the hills. We came back into view as she went to the top of the rolling hills. We kept the rhythm all around the course, taking every jump in stride. At the end, we did well. Peach got pats on her velvety soft neck, and she did her little crow hops, to show her excitement.

The last rider finished the course. We waited for the announcement of the winning numbers over the loud speaker. I held my breath, imagining we won. *This is taking forever. I wonder if the judge can't decide who should win.* Finally, we heard: "First place, Fleet Nancy owned and ridden by Deanie Humphrys."

I trotted Peach out in front of the judge, Mr. Johnson. "She's a special horse. You'd better not let anything happen to her. Ain't nothin' here today that can touch her."

"Thank you, Mr. Johnson. We'll take good care of her, don't worry."

We won all three classes that day, which meant we had the most points in our division. We took home a long red, yellow and blue ribbon, and silver bowl. Imagine... we are champions for the first time ever. *Peach is flapping her lip. She looks especially pretty wearing the championship ribbon.*

Peach ate her oats that night from the silver bowl and she got a nice rest for a few days. "Do the oats taste better when you eat them out of the silver bowl, Peach? I bet they're even yummier than usual. Thanks for being the most amazing horse in the universe." I kissed her nose.

Dark N Fancy relaxing at home

Do you know what Peach liked to do for fun? She rolled in the sand. Horses love that, especially after you worked hard to groom them. Guess what else Peach enjoyed? She liked visiting her favorite friend, Holly's pony Dark N Fancy, her boyfriend. She must've liked the short, dark and handsome type. They made a cute couple. He was black, with white socks on all four legs, and an uneven white blaze on his head. She might have been impressed with his talent, because he was an excellent jumper with courage and style. Holly took Dark N Fancy to the same shows as Peach and I entered, but in different events.

Dark N Fancy

Handsomeness and jumping talent weren't Dark N Fancy's only talents. Holly taught him tricks. He would bow when she asked him. He would also rub her cheek when she said, "Give me a kiss." He loved the carrot rewards afterward.

Sometimes Peach would be out in the riding ring relaxing. What happened if she saw Dark N Fancy grazing in the pasture? She jumped the fence so they could play together.

Holly, Dark N Fancy jumping

Chapter 21: Big Wins at Sleepy Village

We decided to enter a show at Sleepy Village Club in New York. This time we were bringing Dark N Fancy, Peach, and some of our other horses, so we needed the big yellow horse van. Peach got her customized space in the center of the floor for the long trip. My sister, Terri, was sharing Peach with me by riding her in a different division, called Amateur Owner, for riders who were not professionals.

We arrived with barely enough time to practice a few jumps before the start of the show, but we wanted to give

Peach a little exercise before her classes because she was entered in several events.

Holly and Dark N Fancy were fantastic, winning all the pony events. We cheered wildly from the sidelines. Dark N Fancy won Pony Hunter Champion that day, earning a long ribbon and beautiful trophy. Dark N Fancy proved Peach wasn't the only good jumper in the family. He showed he was not afraid of any jump. What a great team he and Holly made.

Peach must've wanted to keep up with her boyfriend, Dark N Fancy, because she won all of her classes with me, and with Terri. That means Peach won Open Hunter Champion and Amateur Owner Championships. This was a big event to celebrate so we decided to stop at Tarrytown Restaurant for a snack before heading home. Terri drove the van. When she turned to leave the parking lot, it stalled and refused to restart. What a dilemma.

We called the club where the show was held and asked if they had stalls for seven horses for the night. The barn manager said yes. We rode them through the streets very late at night on the way back to the country club. We saw a man leaving a bar. He rubbed his eyes because he couldn't believe the sight of a parade of horses walking down the road in the wee hours of the morning.

I called Mom to ask if I could stay in the barn with Peach, but she said no. I wanted to watch over Peach because she stayed in a strange place. All of the riders rode home with their parents after the eventful day.

After the van was repaired the next day, we brought the horses home. I welcomed Peach home with carrots and kisses on her nose.

Chapter 22: Big Changes and New Plans

You probably know parents want their children to be as close to perfect as possible. With this in mind, my parents took me to the Metropolitan Hospital in New York to see Dr. Benjamin. They wondered if he would have some new treatment or new surgery to improve my walking. He recommended major surgery on my right leg and hip. He said he could reposition my leg and hipbone so when it healed, it would be much straighter. The surgery would involve a lot of discomfort. I'd need to learn to use crutches, but the doctor felt it would make a big difference in my walking. My parents and I talked about it for quite a while.

I never had a big surgery or used crutches. What will it be like? The hospital is in New York City, a big confusing place. I know Mom hates driving in busy traffic so either Daddy or Terri would drive there and back.

"Daddy, how long do you think it will be until I can ride again?"

"The doctor said it would take a year, but I think you can do it sooner. You'll be able to walk much better. When your right leg heals, you'll ride better than ever."

I'll walk more like other people. I'll recover faster than anyone. The doctor said I'd be in the hospital for two weeks. My goal is to come home in ten days. I couldn't imagine being away from Peach for that long.

After careful thought, we all agreed surgery was the best option. I counted the days before the surgery. I couldn't sleep the night before we left. Mom packed my little suitcase with nightgowns, books and crossword puzzles. She added my fuzzy pink slippers. Daddy, Mom and I got into the car and went down the driveway. I turned to look at the house. Frost covered some of the windows. It's good there's no snow today. Driving in the city with snow and ice must be dreadful.

———⟡———

Mom and Daddy walked me to my room at the hospital. There were two beds. A young lady sat in the other bed. "Hi, I'm Irene," she said.

"Hi, my name is Deanie."

Mom put my clothes in the closet and sat on the bed. "Everything will be fine, honey. You'll do great and we'll call you tomorrow night and come by to see you the next day." She and Daddy kissed and hugged me. Mom was getting teary-eyed so she turned to leave, hoping I wouldn't notice.

The surgery took three and a half hours. When I woke up the nurse said, "Your operation is all over, honey. The doctor will come talk to you in a minute."

I mumbled, "My leg hurts." *Wasn't that a silly thing to say? Of course it's going to hurt.*

"I'll get something to help the pain," she said. The nurse came back and gave me a shot into my leg, ouch.

Before I fell asleep, Dr. Benjamin came by. "Hi Deanie, the surgery went well. I'm happy with the results."

Mom and Daddy called the day after the surgery. Mom talked first. "Hi, honey. How are you feeling?"

"I'm okay. My leg feels a little better today than last night. The nurse came in to give me a shot of pain stuff in my leg. I hate that, but it made me feel better."

"Every day you'll feel better, dear. Keep up the good work. Daddy wants to talk to you now."

"Hi Honey, how are you doing?"

"I'm okay, Daddy. I got out of bed this afternoon. I walked a couple of steps using a walker. Most of the time I'm sleepy, but Dr. Benjamin said tomorrow I'll start therapy. I hope it's not too hard. How is Peach?"

"Good girl, I'm glad you're out of bed already. Peach is doing well. I'm sure she misses you, though. We let her out to play today. She had fun running and bucking in the snow."

I started physical therapy to learn to use crutches. It was harder than I expected. My left leg crossed in front of the right one and tripped me. It annoyed me. I fell and had to have an X-ray to make sure nothing happened to my right leg. Luckily, it was okay.

Dr. Benjamin came in after the therapy session. "I'm sorry you fell. I didn't expect you to have as much trouble learning to use crutches. We'll schedule more therapy for you so you're more comfortable with them," he said.

Mom and Daddy, came every other day. Daddy walked with me in the halls. "Good work, honey. Keep it up. You're getting stronger all the time. Today your left leg didn't get in the way."

Sometimes Terri and Holly came, too. Terri helped with driving. Holly thought the coolest thing in my room was the electric bed. She giggled the first time she saw how many things you could do with it just by pushing the button.

Mom said, "Dr. Benjamin showed me your X-ray today. Yikes, if I knew he was going to put metal stuff in your leg to hold the bone, maybe I'd have told him not to do it."

"It's okay, Mom. Maybe it looks worse than it is. My leg feels much better than in the beginning."

I walked in the halls as often as I could. It tired me, but my skills with the crutches improved. Finally, on the tenth day the doctor came to visit me.

"I'm still worried about you using the crutches. I'm not sure you are ready to go home," he said.

I felt disappointed but not ready to give up.

"Did you know I've been practicing as much as I can? Besides, you know fish makes you smarter. I'll eat fish every day when I get home and that'll make me so smart I'll be good at using the crutches."

Hooray! He said I could go home. I can't wait to see Peach again. I miss her so much.

⟶◦⟵

I was dressed and ready when Mom and Daddy came to take me home. "I'm surprised you're all ready to leave," Daddy said.

We got in the car and started for home. The streets are so crowded in the city. Daddy almost missed the turn to take us back to Connecticut, but we made it.

Daddy parked the car in front of the steps by the main entrance. Daddy helped me climb the steps. Home at last. *I'm excited. When can I see Peach?* Terri and Holly were waiting by the door.

"Welcome home," they said. "We missed you."

"Thanks, it's good to be back."

"Let me help you to your room, honey. You should take a nap after the long trip," Mom said.

I looked at my room. My eyes widened. "Oh, Mom, my room looks beautiful. I love the new pink walls and the new rug. Thank you so much."

"Daddy and I wanted to give you a surprise for a welcome home present."

"After my nap," I said. "Can I see Peach now?"

"Sure, Holly will go to the barn and bring her to your window," Daddy said.

I sat by the fieldstone fireplace and waited for Peach and Holly. In a few minutes, I saw them. Peach was wearing her warm maroon and gold winter blanket. She looked at me through the window. Seeing her made me smile.

Chapter 23: The Plan

Terri agreed to ride and show Peach while I recovered from the surgery. We didn't want Peach sitting around with nowhere to go. She would've been bored stiff. If we chose the shows carefully, Peach could become the Connecticut High Score Award winner for the Amateur Owner Hunter Division. It's an award for winning the most points in the state of Connecticut. We entered the shows that gave us the opportunity to win the most points toward the award. The horse with the most points in each division would win the award at the end of the year.

Peach and Terri entered five shows that year and won championships in most of them. I watched, even when I used crutches or a cane. Every ribbon we won added more points toward the award. A championship or reserve championship, added even more to our total. Peach and Terri were a team to admire.

The first show Peach and Terri entered was quite far away, nearly in Massachusetts. We were up super early to allow plenty of time of traveling. Peach had pretty braids in her mane. Wearing her soft blue bandages to protect her legs, Terri took Peach out of her stall and walked her on the trailer. But before she could fasten Peach in, she backed up and ran around the yard. It was dark. We discovered how difficult it was to track down a black horse in the dark. But fortunately, she galloped back into her stall after she romped around the yard. Peach's little unplanned adventure made us leave later than we planned. Maybe she felt guilty because she won every class that day. She was happy all day, crow hopping after every class.

One of the most exciting shows Peach and Terri entered was at the Hunter's Club summer show. It was a huge event, with several days of competition. When Terri drove the trailer through the entrance, we saw hundreds of horse vans and trailers from all over the country. There were colorful striped tents everywhere. Peach looked around when she got off the trailer. She flapped her lip. Maybe she knew it was a big day. Terri practiced a few jumps on the flat beautiful course. Peach shook her head and crow hopped. She was ready to get to work.

"Everyone in the Amateur Owner Hunter Class please come to the field," said the announcer.

Terri and Peach waited patiently for their turn. The announcer called, "Our next competitor is Fleet Nancy, ridden by Terri Humphrys."

Peach galloped to the first jump. She jumped it perfectly. Every jump was spectacular. Peach bounced up and down at the end, to celebrate her good work. Terri patted Peach's neck. Now we had to wait. It took ages to come to the end of the class because over eighty horses entered. Finally, we heard...

"Ladies and gentlemen our second-place winner is Fleet Nancy, ridden by Terri Humphrys."

Holly and I clapped and cheered from the bleachers. Peach looked gorgeous with the big red ribbon on her bridle. "Good girl, Peach. You were amazing today," I said, kissing her nose.

Before the next class started, it rained. The field was covered in gooey mud. Nearly every jump was good, but Peach slid going into the gate jump, so the take-off to the jump was not quite as good as the others. Still, she did well. Terri patted her neck, while Holly and I clapped from the bleachers.

When Terri finished, she said, "The mud made the field sticky. Peach's hooves were like suction cups in it, yuck. She still did pretty well. I had to keep encouraging her with my legs to give her confidence."

After another long wait, the announcer said, "And the fourth-place ribbon goes to "Fleet Nancy, ridden by Terri Humphrys."

<hr />

When we got home from the show at the Hunter's Club, Daddy got a phone call from someone with a big show stable in North Carolina. He said he watched Peach at the Hunter's Club show. He was so impressed he wanted to buy her for any amount Daddy wanted. Of course, Daddy said, "Thank you, she's an amazing horse, but she belongs to my daughter and I don't know how I'd replace her." It's a good thing Daddy said no. I couldn't imagine life without Peach.

<hr />

What do you think happened at the end of the year? Peach earned one hundred sixty-eight points, seven more than the second-place horse. That means Peach won the Connecticut award for the most points in her division. There was a special banquet celebration for the winners of the different divisions. It was exciting to wear my first fancy dress to the special event. Mom took me to an exclusive shop to buy something especially pretty for the banquet. We won a beautiful engraved plaque with Peach's name on it.

Peach makes me feel luckier than anyone. She is a shining star. Imagine how far she's come since she lived on the farm in Ohio.

Chapter 24: Together Again

Six months after my surgery I still used a cane. When I walked, it felt different than before. I learned to use muscles that had never worked before. It seemed to take forever to get everything right, but my leg and foot were straighter. Everyone noticed the improvement.

One morning Daddy said, "What do you think about riding Peach today?"

"I can try. I don't know what my leg will feel like."

"I think you're ready. You never know what you can do until you try."

When I got on Peach the first time, I was stunned. My leg wouldn't do anything. I couldn't move it close to the saddle.

Yikes! My leg won't move. What happens if it's always like this? I couldn't imagine not riding as well as before.

I didn't spend much time on Peach that day, because I could only walk around.

When I arrived back in the house after riding, Mom took one look at me and asked, "What happened dear?"

"My leg wouldn't work. There was a big space between my leg and the saddle. My leg flopped around in the air. I couldn't do anything with it. It was horrible."

"Don't worry, honey. Your muscles will get stronger. It hasn't been long since your surgery. You can't expect your leg to be strong the first day back."

Mom always knew how to cheer me up. If I had a bad day with Peach, she'd make chicken for dinner because it was my favorite. She'd be the first to offer hugs and kisses, because they always lifted my spirits when things seemed to be falling apart.

"Okay," I said, choking back the tears. "I'll try to give it more time."

I practiced every day and my leg got stronger gradually. *What a relief. My leg works again.* Eventually, we tried jumping and things seemed to be back to normal.

Sometimes when I taught small riding classes, I'd ride Peach at the same time. It was fun and we both kept in shape that way. At the end of the class, when the students were cooling their horses off, Peach and I practiced jumping. One night, two of the students asked me to jump and they set up something sizeable. It was a crossrail under a big post and rail jump. It was four feet, nine inches, almost as tall as I am.

I cantered Peach in a circle, maintaining the speed I felt best. Her ears pricked forward. She looked ahead at the jump. I didn't feel afraid. Without hesitation, she sailed over the jump and crow hopped at the end to show she had fun. I patted her velvety neck and she pushed it against my hand, letting me know more pats were better than a few. She earned extra carrots that night and a special rub down. I bandaged her legs to protect them after the hard work they did. *We're back. We'll be ready for the shows.*

We left the jump up so I could show Daddy what we jumped. When he looked at it, he said,

"Oh, my gosh. It's amazing you jumped that only nine months after your surgery."

"She was perfect, Daddy. You would have been so proud of us."

I showed him her hoofprints in the dirt so he could see exactly where she left the ground.

"Wow, it must've been some jump."

I couldn't argue with that.

Chapter 25: Spotlight

"Daddy, can you take us to the show at Mrs. Foster's Farm this weekend? We've been doing well in practice. I think we're ready. The jumps will be three feet six inches, but that's what we normally jump."

"I don't see why not. We'll see what you can do in the first show after the surgery."

"Thanks Daddy, I can't wait."

Peach was so shiny, she practically glowed when we left for Mrs. Foster's Farm. Her braids were evenly spaced along her neck. Wearing her blue bandages, she trotted along behind me toward the trailer, flapping her lip along the way.

When we arrived at the show grounds, riders were bustling around the course. The tall grass tangled around my boots, making walking difficult.

It was our turn to jump the course. Daddy gave me a kiss for luck before I made the circle approaching the first jump. *Good, the hedge jump was perfect. We need to take one jump at a time. Don't get anxious.*

Everything went smoothly. There were three jumps left. Suddenly, my right foot slipped out of the stirrup. This was not time to panic. *Don't think about the stirrup.*

We finished the course and everything felt fine. Whew! We waited for the announcement of the winners.

"First place: number 97, Fleet Nancy, owned and ridden by Deanie Humphrys."

After the winners were announced, someone hollered, "Would you like me to jog her out, honey?" thinking it would be hard for me to manage running in the wet, tangled grass with my horse. "Jogging her out," means leading Peach in a trot, in front of the judge, so he can see she's not limping. If she had been limping, we would have broken the rules and someone else would've won first place.

"Thanks, but I've been waiting all day to jog her. I can do it." I trotted her onto the field, careful not to trip in the grass.

I kissed Peach's velvety soft brown nose. She nuzzled my pocket, sniffing the carrots in it. She knew we were a winning team. We earned the Reserve Championship that day, collecting the second highest number of points in our events.

Peach and Deanie, Reserve Champions, Mrs. Foster's Farm
Photo Courtesy of Bob Moseder Photography

The show at Oxford Farm, in Connecticut, was one of the biggest in the country. I felt confident after the show at Mrs. Foster's Farm. Were we ready for an even bigger show?

"Daddy, can we go to Oxford Farm this weekend? I'd like to see how we measure up in one of the biggest shows around. Maybe we'll just try one class and see how it goes."

"Sure, we'll give it a shot," he said.

The day came and I was in my usual nervous state. Peach looked gorgeous, perfectly groomed and braided. When we arrived, the fields were dotted with portable stables and concession tents. Horses and trailers filled every available space. The weather made me more anxious. Sheets of water were pouring down. I had my raincoat and leather gloves, but it was chilly and uncomfortable at best.

My class started. I watched the riders splash around in the slippery mud. Some people decided to "scratch" or not go in the class, but dozens of soggy riders waited their turn. Daddy felt we should be able to compete in any kind of weather so scratching wasn't an option. *It's so muddy in there it looks like a swamp. Maybe we'll see frogs and lily pads while we're jumping.*

"I'm next, Daddy."

"You'll be fine," he said reassuringly. "Just ride her like you always do."

"Okay, we'll try," I said, giving him a last-minute kiss.

We entered the ring and galloped toward the first jump. Mud splashed everywhere. My reins slipped. The first jump was just right. *It's not that bad. Peach feels fine. It doesn't seem like she's stuck in the mud yet.* We continued to the second jump. I thought she was ready to take it in stride, but she snuck in a short step. We continued and the other jumps were good. I gave Peach pats at the end. She deserved them. We were almost perfect. We didn't win that day, but I felt we belonged competing against the best. Nobody wins every time. We put in our best effort. Was I disappointed? Of course, but the world didn't end. I still had the family I loved. I still had Peach.

Deanie Humphrys-Dunne

Chapter 26: Missing in the Storm

Mom and Daddy rolled down the driveway in the motorhome we called the jolly green giant. I didn't expect to see them for at least three weeks. They were driving to Mexico to see Mr. and Mrs. Nesmith, who had moved there a few months earlier. Things went smoothly on the farm until that afternoon. The morning lessons were on schedule. After lunch, I went back to the barn, looking for Peach and Dark N Fancy. They had been relaxing together in the paddock, but now they were gone. I searched the fields, the barns, and every nook and cranny where I thought they might hide, but they were nowhere to be found. I asked our frail, elderly caretaker, Jack, if he had seen the two missing horses. "Nope, they're probably in the barn," he said.

"I looked already, Jack, they're gone. I'll take two lead ropes and a bucket of oats. I'll walk across the street to the Dorfman's. Maybe the horses are in the apple orchard. If I don't see them, I'll start walking down the road." I walked across to the Dorfman's gorgeous stone estate. There were tennis courts, and gardens galore, but they had a grumpy gardener. I saw him trimming the bushes. "Excuse me, sir, have you seen a black horse and a black pony with a blaze?"

"No, I haven't and I have more to do than chase after your horses," he grumbled.

I hurried away and walked down the road. I saw someone walking her dog. "Have you seen a black horse and a black pony with a white blaze?"

"No, I'm sorry. I haven't seen them. I hope you find them before the weather worsens."

It started raining hard and the wind increased. This weather was no fun. A few cars went by. Some of the drivers stopped to ask if they could help. I explained what I was doing and thanked them. By now I'd been walking for a long time, but there was still no sign of the horses. *At least I have my rain gear on, but I'm feeling soggy and tired. Where could they be?*

Meanwhile back at the farm, a family friend, Mr. Roberts, stopped by to check in on me. He'd known us for years. I called him Uncle Joe. He'd promised Mom and Daddy he'd come from time to time while they were away. He asked Jack if I was around.

"Nope, she went lookin' for Peach and Holly's pony. Don't know where they've gone off to."

"Okay, I'll get in my car and see if I can find her."

I'd tromped all the way to the next town and hadn't seen the horses yet. The poor things must be cold and drenched. *I wish they'd show up.* Just as I was about to give up hope, I looked near the bushes at the side of the road. I saw them eating the wildflowers, trying to look innocent. I offered Peach some oats from the bucket and she happily ate her share. I snapped the lead rope onto her halter. "You rascal, I should be mad at you, but you couldn't let your boyfriend run off without you." Rainwater dripped from my hat into the pail. Dark N Fancy pushed Peach's head out of the way to claim his share of the snack. I attached the other lead rope to the pony's halter. We turned around, headed for home.

A few minutes later I saw Uncle Joe's car. He stuck his head out the window. "Hey, I've been looking for you. I'll tie the horses to the back of my minivan. Hop in the car. We'll get you and the horses out of this weather." We hugged when I sat down. "How are you feeling after all that walking?"

"My leg hurts. That happens when I walk a lot."

"Thanks, for being my hero today. You're definitely the best thing I've seen this afternoon. How did you know where I was?"

"I was working near Sweetbrier so I dropped by to see you. Jack told me what happened." Uncle Joe drove slowly, while I kept an eye on Peach and Dark N Fancy. I called Holly to let her know what happened and that we were on our way home.

Holly waited inside the barn. "You naughty boy, running off like that," she said. "Let's get you dried off and tucked into your stall where you'll stay out of trouble."

I dried Peach off and put her in her stall. Thank heavens we were home.

Pearls of Wisdom

Do you know what the word "perseverance" means? The definition of that word is "not giving up." I believe it's the key to achieving your dreams. We often tend to give up when things become difficult. But is that the right choice? Suppose I'd given up when I was learning to jump. Do you think I'd have become a champion? I don't. Instead, it is wise to use your challenges to motivate you toward your goals because when you've conquered one obstacle, you gained the confidence to tackle your next challenge.

What if you wanted to realize one dream, but something happened to prevent the outcome you anticipated? At first, you might feel crushed. You might only think of the sting of the disappointment. Sometimes it means you have other talents you need to develop.

I love motivating you. Every day I look for new things to share with you and ways to inspire you.

Whatever your dream is, reach for it and persevere, because you may accomplish more than you ever imagined. You may even beat the odds like I did.

Take the Quiz

Take this little quiz and see how well you remember the details of the story.

1. Why did Deanie's Dad decide to teach her to ride horses?
2. What was the name of the Humphrys' family farm?
3. What was the name of Deanie's first pony?
4. What did Little Man like to do when Deanie was riding him?
5. What was the name of Deanie's special horse that her dad bought for her? Do you remember her nickname?
6. What do you think is the main thing Deanie wants you to remember from this story?
7. Why did Peach have to wear pads under her shoes?
8. Who was Peach's "boyfriend?"
9. What was the name of the pony Holly trained to pull a cart?
10. What other things did Holly and her tiny pony like to do?

Quiz Answers

1. Deanie's Dad thought learning to ride would help Deanie's legs get stronger so she could walk.

2. The farm was called Sweetbrier.

3. His name was Little Man

4. He liked to fall asleep. Not a very nice trick, was it?

5. Fleet Nancy, but her nickname was Peach.

6. Deanie wants children to remember never to give up on their dreams because anything is possible if you don't give up.

7. Peach needed pads under her shoes because her feet were sensitive after the mystery sickness.

8. Peach's boyfriend was Dark N Fancy.

9. The name of Holly's pony who pulled the cart was Goldie.

10. Holly and Goldie liked to play pony express.

Deanie Humphrys-Dunne

About the Author

Deanie Humphrys-Dunne is an award-winning children's author. She is a graduate of the Institute of Children's Literature and has been featured on several author websites. Her books have won a number of awards and recognition including; The Feathered Quill silver medal, The Purple Dragonfly Honorable Mention, CLIPPA finalist, Reader's Favorite silver medal, and The AuthorsShow.com "50 Great Writers You Should Be Reading."

Her story, *My Life at Sweetbrier,* is a captivating book that teaches children life lessons such as perseverance and setting goals. Deanie believes every child should be inspired to reach for their dreams because they may accomplish more than they imagine. You may even beat the odds, like she did.

Deanie's sister, Holly Humphrys-Bajaj, has beautifully illustrated four of Deanie's fictional books: *Charlie the Horse, Charlene the Star, Charlene the Star and Hattie's Heroes,* and *Charlene the Star and Bentley Bulldog.*

For more about Deanie and Holly, visit...

www.childrensbookswithlifelessons.com

Made in the USA
Middletown, DE
23 November 2019